THE STORY OF MOSES

Publishers Since 1798

THOMAS NELSON PUBLISHERS
Nashville

First published in 1994 by
Thomas Nelson Publishers, Nashville, Tennessee.

Copyright © 1994 Bluewood Books

Story retold by Bill Yenne

Art and design direction by Bill Yenne. Illustrated by Mark Busacca, Edwin Esquivel, Emi Fukawa, Victor Lee, Doug Scott, Vadim Vahrameev, Hanako Wakiyama, and Bill Yenne. Special thanks to Ruth DeJauregui.

Produced by
Bluewood Books (A Division of The Siyeh Group, Inc.)
P.O. Box 460313, San Francisco, CA 94146

Yenne, Bill, 1949-
    The Story of Moses/[story retold for this edition by Bill Yenne].
        p.   cm.—(Children's Bible Classics)
    ISBN 0-7852-8325-0 (MM)—ISBN 0-7852-8329-3 (TR)
    1. Moses (Biblical leader)—Juvenile literature. 2. Bible stories, English—O.T. Exodus. [1. Moses (Biblical leader) 2. Bible Stories—O.T.] I. Title. II. Series.
BS580.M6Y465 1994
222'.1209505—dc20   93-37476
                                                                CIP
                                                                AC

96 97 98— 2 3 4 5

Printed and bound in the United States of America

THE STORY OF MOSES

Long ago, there was a famine in the land of Israel, and the people went to live in the land of Egypt. They found very rich soil in Egypt, and they could grow three or four crops every year. These Hebrew people stayed in Egypt for many years, but they lived apart from the people of Egypt. They worshipped God and stayed away from Egyptian idols.

The Egyptian king, called Pharaoh, saw that there were a lot of Israelites. He was afraid there would soon be more Israelites than there were Egyptians.

He said to his people, "Let us rule these Israelites more strictly. They might turn against us one day."

He made the Israelites work for the Egyptians and build cities for them. But still Pharaoh thought there were too many Israelites. He decided to kill all the baby boys born to the Israelites.

One Hebrew mother wanted to save her baby boy. She put the baby in a small basket and sent his sister Miriam to watch as the basket floated down the river. Pharaoh's daughter saw the basket floating on the water among the reeds when she went to bathe. She opened it and there was a beautiful little Israelite baby. The princess saw Miriam and said to her, "Go find an Israelite woman to take care of the baby."

Miriam went and brought the baby's own mother to the princess. The princess told the mother, "Take this child to your home and nurse him for me, and I will pay you for it."

The baby's mother was happy! No one could hurt her baby son now because he was protected by the princess of Egypt.

When the boy was older, Pharaoh's daughter took him to live in the palace. She named him "Moses," a name that means "to take out," because she had taken him out of the water.

So Moses, the Hebrew boy, lived as the son of the princess in the palace. Even though Moses grew up among the Egyptians, he still loved his own people. The Israelites were poor slaves who served the Lord God.

Moses grew angry with the way the Egyptians mistreated the Israelites. One day he killed an Egyptian. Pharaoh heard about it and Moses ran away. For many years, Moses lived alone in the desert with his flocks. Meanwhile, the people of Israel were working as slaves in Egypt.

One day Moses was watching his father-in-law's animals when he saw a bush on fire. He watched to see the fire burn it up, but the bush kept burning.

Moses heard a voice coming out of the bush, calling him by name. "Moses, Moses! I am the God of your father, the God of Abraham and of Isaac and of Jacob. I have seen how My people suffer in Egypt, and I have heard their cry. I am coming to free them and to bring them up to the Promised Land. You will lead My people out of Egypt. Go and tell them what I have said. Then tell Pharaoh to let My people go."

Moses asked God to give him some sign which he could show the people to prove that God had sent him. God told him to throw his shepherd's staff on the ground.

Moses threw it down. It turned into a snake, and God said, "Take hold of it by the tail."

When Moses did, it again became a staff in his hand.

God said to Moses, "If they will not believe you when you speak My words, show them this sign."

But Moses said, "Oh, Lord, I am not a good speaker."

And God said, "I will teach you what to say."

Aaron, who was Moses' brother, came to meet Moses. God told Moses he would make Aaron the spokesman and Moses would perform the miracles. Together, they went to the people of Israel.

After Moses and Aaron told the Hebrews what God said, they went to see Pharaoh.

"The Lord God of Israel has told us to take our people out of Egypt," they told Pharaoh. "God says, 'Let My people go.'"

Pharaoh was very angry. He said he would not let the Hebrews go. Instead, Pharaoh made the people work even harder.

The Hebrews were upset with Moses and Aaron for making their suffering worse.

Moses and Aaron went back to Pharaoh and again asked him in the Lord's name to let the people go. Pharaoh laughed. "Who is the Lord? Why should I obey His commands? What sign can you show me?"

Aaron threw down his staff, and it turned into a snake. But Pharaoh called his Egyptian wise men and magicians. They threw down their staffs which became snakes, too. But Aaron's staff, in the form of a snake, swallowed them all.

Moses warned Pharaoh that God's punishment, called plagues, would come if he refused to obey God's command. God turned all the water into blood, but Pharaoh *still* would not obey. Then Aaron stretched out his staff and all the land was covered with *frogs*!

Pharaoh said, "Pray to your God for me. Ask Him to take the frogs away, and I will let your people go."

Moses prayed, and God took away the frogs. But after the plague was gone, Pharaoh broke his promise and still held the people as slaves.

God then sent plagues of lice, flies, locusts, deadly animal disease, sickness, hailstorms and darkness. Each time Pharaoh asked Moses to take the plague away. He said he would let the Israelites go, but each time he lied.

God said to Moses, "There will be one more plague, and then Pharaoh will be glad to let the people go. He will drive you out of the land. Get your people ready to leave Egypt."

Moses told his people that at midnight, the Angel of the Lord would go through the land. The oldest child in every house would die unless they found a lamb, killed it, and put the lamb's blood on the frame around the door of each house. They were to roast the lamb and eat it quickly, so they could be ready to march away as soon as the meal was over.

The Israelites did as Moses commanded them. This supper was called "Passover" because when the Angel saw the doors sprinkled with blood, he *passed over* those houses and did not enter them.

As the Angel of the Lord moved through the land, all the people of Egypt became scared. Pharaoh sent a messenger to Moses and Aaron. He said, "Go, get out of Egypt! Take everything that you own. Pray to your God to bless me also."

The Israelites left in a great hurry. To show them the way, God went in front of them in the form of a pillar of clouds during the day and as a pillar of fire at night.

In a few days, the Hebrews came to the shore of the Red Sea. The water was in front of them and high mountains were on each side of them.

Meanwhile, Pharaoh became angry that he had let them go because now he didn't have any slaves. He ordered his army to bring them back.

The Hebrews were upset with Moses. They said, "Why did you bring us out into this terrible place? We are surrounded by the mountains and the sea and our enemies are close behind us. It would be better to be slaves in Egypt than to die here in the wilderness!"

"Do not be afraid," Moses said. "God will save you." Moses held out his hand over the sea. A mighty east wind blew over the sea and divided the water. The Hebrews crossed the sea on a strip of dry land.

When the Egyptians saw the Hebrews marching across dry ground, they followed with their horses and their chariots. But the ground was soft and their chariot wheels got stuck and their horses fell down. The Egyptians became frightened. Moses held out his hand and the sea closed in on them.

God saved all the Hebrews from the Egyptians. Soon they found themselves in a strange land that they had never seen before. This was the land of Sinai where Moses had seen God in the burning bush.

The Israelites traveled for many days through the hot desert until they came to Mount Sinai. God provided everything they needed. They had enough bread, meat and water. Some time later, Moses went up on to the mountain to speak with God.

Moses wanted to find out what God expected him to do next. At last he heard God's voice say, "Moses, if the people of Israel keep My commandments, they will be My chosen people."

God gave Moses the ten laws He wanted His people to keep.

God wrote these commandments on stone tablets with His own finger and gave them to Moses.

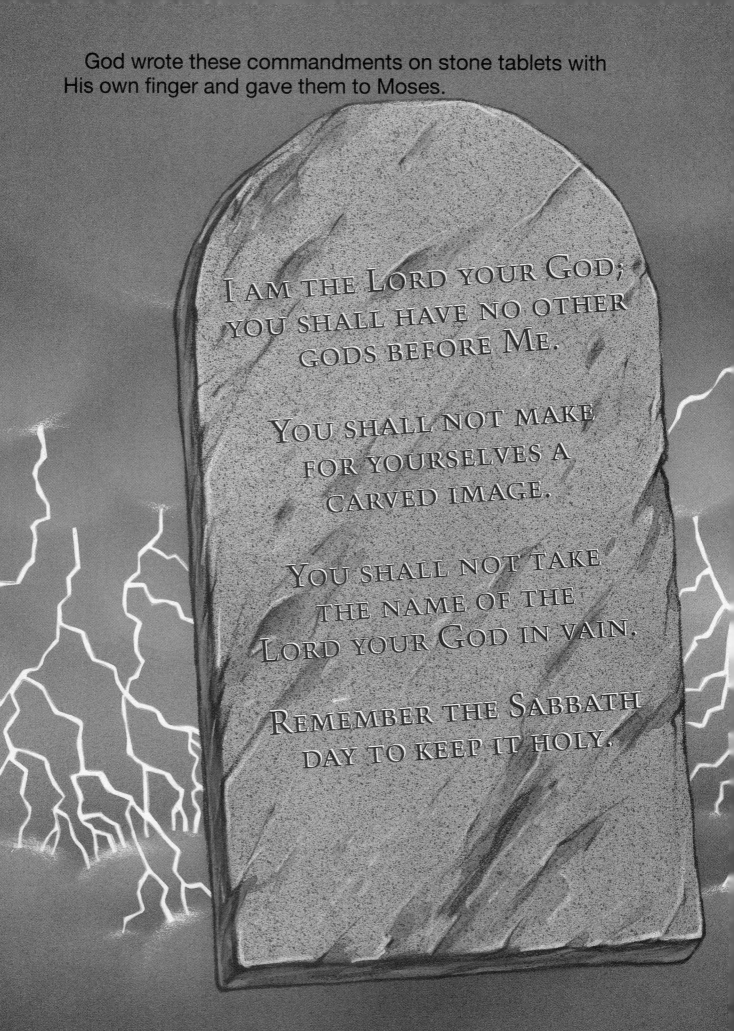

I AM THE LORD YOUR GOD; YOU SHALL HAVE NO OTHER GODS BEFORE ME.

YOU SHALL NOT MAKE FOR YOURSELVES A CARVED IMAGE.

YOU SHALL NOT TAKE THE NAME OF THE LORD YOUR GOD IN VAIN.

REMEMBER THE SABBATH DAY TO KEEP IT HOLY.

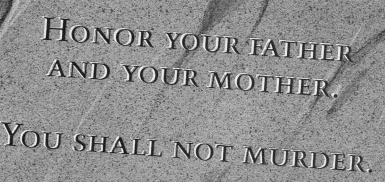

HONOR YOUR FATHER
AND YOUR MOTHER.

YOU SHALL NOT MURDER.

YOU SHALL NOT COMMIT
ADULTERY.

YOU SHALL NOT STEAL.

YOU SHALL NOT BEAR FALSE
WITNESS AGAINST YOUR
NEIGHBOR.

YOU SHALL NOT COVET
ANYTHING THAT IS YOUR
NEIGHBOR'S.

When Moses brought down the tablets, he saw that the people had built an altar to a golden calf. Instead of worshipping God, they were worshipping animals like the Egyptians.

Moses was so angry that he smashed the tablets containing the commandments of God. Then he took the calf and burned it and ground it into powder.

The people of Israel were sorry and accepted God's commandments. God provided Moses with two more tablets to put in a special box called the Ark of the Covenant. Wherever the children of Israel stayed, the Ark was always placed in the middle of the camp.

They took the Ark with them as they marched out across the desert again, and they kept it with them until Moses led them to the Promised Land many years later.